WHAT SHOULD THE SCHOOLS TEACH?

by Fred T. Wilhelms,
retired executive secretary,
Association for Supervision and Curriculum Development

Library of Congress Catalog Card Number: 72-93706
Copyright © 1972 by the Phi Delta Kappa Educational Foundation,
Bloomington, Indiana

TABLE OF CONTENTS

WHAT SHOULD SCHOOLS TEACH?

The two main requirements for thinking straight about the whole question of what our schools ought to teach are nerve and common sense, or, to put it a little differently, *the nerve to use common sense.*

If we were talking about methods we could not put such emphasis on common sense, for in the area of methodology there is a considerable body of scientific evidence, and the professionals in education have developed great expertise. But in the area of curricula there is little scientific evidence to go by. The main questions have to do with what we want our schools to produce. Those questions are not reserved for the experts; therefore, a thoughtful common-sense approach is perfectly valid.

The matter of nerve is relevant because it takes courage to shake ourselves loose from comfortable old notions and habits of thought. All of us have come up through a certain kind of school program; some of us have trained ourselves to teach part of that program and have spent years of our lives working at it. It is not at all strange, then, that we come to see the program we are used to as the natural thing. It is difficult to admit that some of the objectives for which we have worked so hard—as learners or as teachers—may not have been worth the effort (or, at least, that something else might have been better). But the blunt fact is that we have accumulated a lot of junk. We have to get rid of it to make room for what really counts—and that takes nerve.

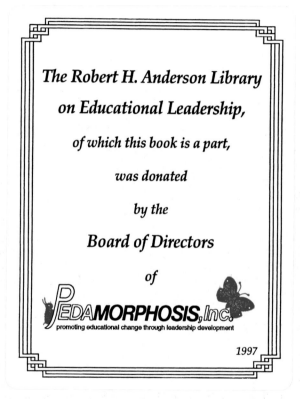

CLEARING THE DECK FOR ACTION

When the old-time captain of a warship knew he was going into battle, he ordered the crew to clear the decks for action. This meant getting out of the way everything that was not absolutely necessary for the fight, but it also meant getting into position everything that *was* essential. In the next few pages, we shall try an exercise like that with reference to the curriculum.

There are a few subjects we absolutely have to have. One group of them is included in the old phrase, "readin' and 'ritin' and 'rithmetic." We have to have these because they are the tools that enable us to handle everything else.

It is true that radio and television and all the graphic arts which we now produce with ease have relaxed our dependence on the printed page. We need to teach the better use of such new media. Still, as far as we can look ahead, the ability to get information, ideas, and enjoyment from written materials will remain fundamental. This does not necessarily mean that we need to devote enormous blocks of time to formal instruction in reading, all by itself, which some people demand. Maybe we can do the job better by weaving reading into other activities in a functional way. One way or another, we must help all children learn to read.

The same is true of writing. It is true that bosses use dictating machines and that secretaries—and many others—use typewriters. Nevertheless, the ability to put thoughts on paper—and that includes much more than the ability to form letters and words—is essential.

Finally, there is the ability to handle numbers and quantities. Let us skip for the moment the higher kinds of mathematics; we can come back to them later. There is a basic kind of arithmetic that has to do with counting, measuring, adding, subtracting, multiplying, dividing, and handling the ordinary transactions of household affairs and business. This much is essential for everybody.

There we have what we might call the bedrock of schooling. It is what the old-time grade schools dealt with almost entirely, and it is the main substance of what are often called literacy programs in underdeveloped nations. From here on, we shall assume, in whatever else we say about the school program, that this foundation will be taken care of well.

From here on we are in an area offering far greater freedom of choice than people generally realize—so much freedom that people sometimes seem frightened to think about it. This does not mean that we have already listed all the essentials there are. Far from it! The freedom lies in the wide choice of methods for getting at most of the essentials. When a trained curriculum specialist works with these problems, two guiding principles are almost like "facts of life" to him.

1. Surprisingly few particular pieces of knowledge and skill must be mastered by everybody in the same form.

This statement often comes as a shock to people, because they think it means students do not have to master knowledge and skill. Obviously, that would be false, for people need a great deal of information and know-how. But they do not all need the same bits. And even if two students need roughly equivalent bodies of information, they may not need it in the same form.

If this still shocks you, try making a list. As you put down each item, check your thinking carefully; ask yourself, "Is this really something everybody needs to know just this way, or is it only something I think it would be nice for everybody to know?" The difference between the two considerations is enormous.

2. Generally, what is truly essential is some big goal, and there may be many different ways of reaching that goal.

For example, one goal may be the idea and belief that democracy is better than autocracy as the basis of organization for our country (or family or church congregation). We want this so firmly fixed in students that it will function automatically; we want it "in their bones." Yet we also want it to be an intelligent, rational choice, based on data and experience. Different teachers use an endless variety of inputs to establish it—facts from history and economics, for example, or impressions from art and literature, along with many kinds of experience in student government, school clubs, and so on. One hopes that the facts and the books and experiences will be remembered, but one really knows that most of them will be forgotten. That is not important, however, so long as the result is a loyal, intelligent citizen.

We have stressed these two guiding principles, which are really two different ways of saying the same thing, because they help us keep our eye on the ball and they give us freedom. When we consider what the schools should teach, it is all too easy to get trapped into thinking only about particular bodies of information as if they were the ends in themselves. Generally speaking, they are not; they are means to an end. We need to think about the purposes we wish to achieve. Then we are free to look around for subject matter and experiences that have the best chance of achieving those purposes with a given group of youngsters. (The phrase "have the best chance" is also important to good curriculum thinking. Few things are sure in curriculum work. We have to calculate what inputs are likeliest to generate the outputs we want. And then, even if we succeed, we rarely know what produced what—or whether the same thing would succeed again in another setting.)

To extend this line of thinking a little, let's look at a few examples of purposes and possible means, and see where they lead us.

1. *It is important that all young people learn to use our language well and communicate effectively.* But does this mean we must have extended work in grammar? (Piles of research say no, grammar does not help speaking and writing very much.) Should all students have a series of courses in English composition and write a theme a week? Would organized public discussion or debate on real, carefully studied problems and issues

9

handle the speech problem better? Would close attention to the formal reports needed in the social studies, sciences, and humanities—at times when the student really has something to say and wants to get it said just right—help writing more? Besides, do years of writing formal themes on meaningless subjects, judged almost entirely on correctness of form, do what we want to do to a child's spontaniety, creativity, and genuine urge to communicate?

In other words, do the media we most commonly use match our objectives? Are there other possibilities that are superior?

2. *It is important that young people learn to use literature, art, and music, not only as a means of lifelong enjoyment, but also as a means toward understanding themselves and others and developing a fine sense of values.* Does this mean that everybody has to appreciate Shakespeare, or Rembrandt, or Mozart? Do they all need to read the same classics together? Do they all need survey courses in American literature? Would it be better if each youngster could be helped to develop and follow his own interests with guidance? Are the great motion pictures less important than the great novels? Is it all right if one student gets excited about architecture and is left cold by paintings, while his neighbor gets hooked on poetry but never catches up to the symphony?

How about using cultured, civilized adults as our model? Among them the range and diversity of tastes and enthusiasms are enormous. "One man's meat is another man's poison"—and nobody criticizes the two because they do not agree. The Romans said *de gustibus non est disputandum* (people ought to quit arguing about tastes!). Isn't it time to start applying that principle in school? Maybe we ought to start relaxing our common requirements, not because we do not care about the basic purpose but because we care about it so much.

But we do not need to answer all these questions right now. The point is that there is a world of difference between deciding on our high-priority purposes, on the one hand, and dictating a particular body of subject matter, on the other. One could go on and on with examples. To take just one more:

3. *We all want the schools to turn out intelligently loyal, patriotic young Americans.* But does that automatically make

three years of American history and a year or so of "American Government" the best use of time? This is a big, important question; billions of dollars and hundreds of millions of man-years of work are involved. Questions of this enormity rarely get raised. That is why we say you have to have the nerve to use your common sense if you are going to rethink what the schools should teach.

But it is hard to think of the whole school program at once. This writer finds that it helps to divide the total into a few major parts, not so much by subject matter as by function. He is particularly concerned with four great streams of purpose that run through the whole curriculum:

Offering a career education

Living with the great technology

Developing effective citizenship

Promoting personal fulfillment.

These may not include absolutely everything which someone, with good reason, may wish to see in the school program. (Remember, we have already specified a sound foundation in the tool subjects.) But these four categories may serve reasonably well to structure the rest of the discussion in this pamphlet.

OFFERING A CAREER EDUCATION

The idea of career education has been brought to public attention in the past couple of years by U.S. Commissioner of Education Sidney P. Marland, who has given it high priority. It is not just another name for vocational education. It includes vocational education, but it represents a much broader conception of what it really takes to help a boy or girl succeed in the economic side of life.

The Vocational Aspect

Vocational education itself is, of course, extremely important. We rarely think of it this way, but education always has been, and still is, heavily vocational. In the days when few young people went beyond elementary education, the grade schools provided exactly the background most of them needed in their work. To be sure, they learned most of their working skills on the job, but the "readin', 'ritin' and 'rithmetic" was fundamental.

In our own day, the most completely vocational institutions are the graduate schools, which train men and women precisely for a professional role. The four-year colleges and universities also carry a heavy vocational load; they prepare some students for graduate work, and they directly train many more, such as teachers. It probably comes as a surprise to many, but the old, highly touted ideal of a general, liberal college education has largely given way to highly technical preparation, even in those fields that are still referred to as the liberal arts. (To this writer, it seems predictable that general, liberal education will become the dominant function of the high school.)

At the next level, a variety of two-year community colleges, junior colleges, and technical schools prepare students for a host of subprofessional but highly skilled vocations. In many cases, the majority of their students may still take the "university-parallel" program to prepare for transfer to a senior college, but their most distinctive feature is a wide variety of technical programs. These institutions have been coming onto the scene at a great rate in recent years, and throughout the seventies they will be the fastest growing segment of American education. A key reason for this is that the types of jobs for which they train students are playing a larger and larger part in the American economy.

One attractive feature is that the path to advanced education can be kept open. If the high school and junior college play their parts wisely, the boy who falls in love with cars can study auto mechanics, and then, if his vision expands, he can move on to become an engineering technician or even a full-fledged automotive engineer. There can be "step-off" points at which he can leave school and make an adequate living in a good job, but none of the programs have to be considered terminal. His future need not be closed off just because he takes vocational work. This is a goal to be greatly cherished.

At the secondary level, the peculiarly American institution known as the comprehensive high school has been succeeding only reasonably well. What it does have by way of vocational education works with moderate success. The students in it are generally purposeful and happy, and there is evidence that they do get jobs (not necessarily the ones they trained for) and have better-than-average job success.

However, we generally fail to see how terribly limited these programs are. Shopwork for boys, commercial courses for girls—these are the backbone of a narrow preparation of middle-middle students for middle-middle jobs. It is commonly thought that vocational education provides for the group with low academic achievement. In most situations nothing could be further from the truth. Such students often cannot make it into the standard vocational programs. They are dumped into the so-called

14

"general" curriculum, unquestionably the most damnable program the schools contain. (In all justice, it must be said that this is not the fault of the vocational teachers. They are asked to train students for jobs that are held by competent people in the real world; they have to select students who can do what the jobs demand.) All in all, there are three major "bugs" in the system.

1. As we have already seen, there is a general lack of vocational programs for students at the lowest ability level. To be more accurate, one should say the group with the "lowest *developed* ability." Many of these students have good native ability, intellectually and practically. Their problem is often one of poor background, or, for some reason, they have been so "turned off" by schooling that they can scarcely read or write or apply themselves systematically to anything. Their attitudes are often negative; they may even feel the situation is hopeless.

Two hopeful facts stand out. First, if these boys and girls can be drawn into something that makes sense to them, perhaps for the first time in their school years, they can be trained to do simple kinds of work and do them well. Some programs for the mentally retarded provide ultimate proof of this. Second, there are jobs waiting for them, despite all the talk about how technical our world has become. Any householder who has tried to get a lawn cared for, windows washed, or housework done will testify to that.

Such jobs may not seem the noblest opportunities in an affluent world, but they represent a decent, independent living. And the opportunities are not all that limited. A good janitor is treated with respect by anyone with common sense, and a hospital orderly contributes something of real value.

One of the best things that could happen in American education would be for every secondary school to abolish the despicable general curriculum and set out to meet the needs of the group now held in custody there. The program we need must get under way in the middle and junior high school years, because many of these students are too disaffected to do anything but drop out—mentally or physically—before the standard vocational programs even start. It is not necessarily the ultimate tragedy if a youngster of low academic ability drops out before he gets a diploma; it *is* a tragedy if he drops out with no means of making his way in the world.

2. At the other end of the scale our high schools are typically neglecting the fast-growing technical job fields. High school faculties tend to divide their students into two groups: the college-bound (meaning, really, those headed for the professions); and the non-college group. They take great care to meet every preparatory need—real or fancied—of the first group; they lump the second group into the vocational or general curricula. In this crude process they largely miss an upper-middle group who could do well in the technical fields.

The lag is an odd one. Our society is becoming increasingly dependent on its technicians. Many wonderful jobs are involved, jobs with good pay, good working conditions, and great independence. Training opportunities are multiplying rapidly, as one state after another builds systems of junior colleges, technical institutes, and multilevel area vocational schools. The modifications needed in the high school program would be modest: a careful guidance system and something like the attention to preparatory requirements now given to the college-and-profession-bound. Yet few areas are so neglected in most systems.

This writer recommends that every faculty and every community take a sober look at this problem of vocational preparation for its upper-middle student group. In some cases, the solution will involve the provision of new and expensive educational institutions, but in others, little is needed except careful thought and planning.

3. Vocational preparation is looked at too often as a matter of schooling, which may require a good deal of money to keep equipment updated. High school principals worry about whether the typewriters and calculating machines in the commercial department are this year's model. It might be better if more of the money and energy went into building cooperative relationships that make use of other people's equipment and provide on-the-job experience in real situations. The school would take the role of coordinator, somewhat as it now does in distributive education.

It is, admittedly, a tremendous task to open up enough opportunities to serve all who need them. Small pilot projects involving a few dozen or a few hundred students have been quite successful; full-scale programs are something else again. But as a nation we have a choice to make, one that must be made more by the public, industrialists, businessmen, and labor leaders than by educators. Do we really mean to keep our young people walled off from the realities of the world of work until some magical day—and then start them working full time? Do we really believe a meaningful program of vocational education can go on *in absentia,* so to speak?

Unemployment among young people is generally at least double that among adults, and there is considerable worry about work attitudes and habits. A country gets about what it pays for. We have been holding young people in enclaves of dependency and irresponsibility, to a degree no other major society ever has. We have made meaningful contact with work uniquely difficult, then we expect a sudden transition from full time in school to full time on the job. The evidence shows that the transition is harder and less effective in the United States than in any other industrial nation.

Confidence and Insight

Underneath the problems that lie inside vocational education, there is an even more fundamental concern. The difference between the winners and the losers in the economic area is not just a matter of the vocational education they have had. It is even more an inward problem. Here is where the deeper concepts of career education come in.

The image that boys and girls develop of themselves and of the possibilities life holds for them is crucial. Most young people know incredibly little about jobs. They may scarcely know what their own father does, or their mother if she works outside the home. Children from the slums or from deprived rural areas, who typically do not travel much, may see few modes of work, none of them very exciting. They may know vaguely about more rewarding jobs, but they are likely to identify these with "other people"—a special class of geniuses or the well-to-do. Many schools and teachers are so preoccupied with academic achieve-

17

ment that they make all but the chosen few feel inadequate. They almost forbid a great many perfectly capable, ordinary kids to aspire to anything out of the ordinary. In the process, they erode away still further the students' already shaky self-confidence, and discourage ambitions that could be realized.

This is all wrong! Virtually all young people are capable of learning to do something well. Far more than is commonly realized have the ability to justify going after really high-grade occupations, if only they can work up the nerve and the ambition to prepare themselves well. After all, one does not need to be a genius to become a good carpenter or machine tool operator—or teacher or accountant.

Schools desperately need ways of getting children and youths acquainted with wide areas of the world of work. Starting in kindergarten and climaxing in the junior high school years, where plans begin to crystallize, they need an ongoing, attractive, informative program. Field trips in the area could acquaint students with various kinds of work at first hand. The programs could utilize motion pictures and T.V. shows, and attractive books, posters, and pamphlets. They could even get each youngster some real exploratory experience in a few kinds of work that catch his interest. More than information is involved. The learners need to get the feel of various kinds of work, and to become excited about one or more kinds. Nothing does more to energize a young man or woman than the feeling that there is "something out there" for them. Nothing sucks the energy out of anybody like the hopeless feeling that he is beaten before he starts.

That is why it is so important for the schools also to feed back information to each student about himself. They need to help him see his strengths. This, too, has to be a long, systematic program, building self-insight step by step. Then we can reasonably hope that many more youngsters—knowing of opportunities, knowing what it takes to use them, and knowing their own powers—will "turn on" and aim for the best they are capable of.

This is the heart of career education. It involves vocational education, but it is much more a matter of what happens inside a growing boy or girl.

The Consumer Side of a Career

The job one chooses sets much of one's life pattern—but by no means all of it. The choices of purchases and of life style are also powerful determinants of the life an individual or family actually achieve.

Here again most young people are grossly ignorant of the possibilities that exist. In the main they tend to take as given the kind of life they are accustomed to. Starting in kindergarten and continuing all the way through high school, they need many opportunities to see the alternatives and the kinds of choices people make. They need chances to think and talk about this problem, with guidance, and to slowly hammer out their own personal set of values and tastes to live by. Each of us forms, over time, a kind of mental standard of living, the quality of life we are willing to work hard for. One does not want a young person's image to be mere daydreaming, but perhaps it is better if it is a bit lofty than if it is too modest. Far more lives are blighted by low self-concepts and low aspirations than by overconfidence.

Such a program, of course, must be backed by competence. Schools can help children and youth learn the practical arts of effective shopping and buying. They can inoculate young people against the wiles of shady advertising. They can teach them to use informative advertising and labeling. They can help them identify honest, competent merchants and sales people, and get maximum help from them in generally pleasant relationships. They can teach young people to budget and manage their money, to use credit wisely, and to get the insurance that meets their needs.

Consumer education can provide a great deal of hard-headed, practical advice that will enable a young family to move ahead, turning its dreams into reality. Every school ought to be getting such help to every student.

And yet, important as this practical foundation is and whether we are talking about the producer (job) side of life or the consumer side, in the final analysis it is how each young person sees himself or herself, and the hopes and plans that build up in the mind that make the greatest difference. Career education is not a subject. It is a set of influences, running through every part of education, and its work is mostly inside the person.

LIVING WITH THE GREAT TECHNOLOGY

Some years ago this writer served as a consultant to an Asian nation. Living in that Eastern culture, he learned a great deal about our Western one. Of course, there were the obvious differences in the way the natives lived and worked, but what struck him most forcefully was the difference in modes of thinking. Time after time, when the group was faced with some question, he saw his Asian colleagues reach their answer in an intuitive flash while he was still trying to figure out what data were needed and how to get them, in order to work through to a rational, logical solution. For the first time in his life he began to see how deeply we Americans are acculturated to a kind of scientific method—even if it is crude—in solving our problems.

This element is essential because we live in a technologically oriented society. Intuition is valuable, too, but our technical system could not exist without scientific precision. In school terms, this is peculiarly the domain of the natural sciences and mathematics, though we use the results far beyond the areas that suggests. Clearly, then, schools must have effective programs of science and mathematics from the first year on. The question is: what kinds of programs, for what purposes?

One purpose is to produce specialists. Our society needs fairly large numbers of specialized scientists, engineers, and mathematicians, along with even more technicians. The specialized training belongs in the colleges and graduate schools, but it is the duty of the common schools to build a sound foundation for those who will go on. This the present curriculum is well-equipped to do. But most students will not go on into such specialties. What do *they* need? Is what they need so different that we must have two different kinds of programs?

These questions are hard to answer. Perhaps we can set down a few guidelines:

1. All of us need to get the feel of the scientific approach: the way scientists form questions, develop hypotheses, gather evidence, reason from their data, test their theories, and so on. We need to get the idea of the systematic inquiry so ingrained in our bones that it will function naturally wherever it fits. We need to learn the scientist's love for the truth, the care he takes to test his conclusions, and his willingness to throw them out if they do not stand up. We need the spirit of free inquiry, the nerve to question anything and venture into the unknown.

2. We all need to be able to live comfortably and competently in a world that is already technologically complex and becoming more so with devastating speed.

3. As a matter of general intelligence we need to be able to read with understanding at least the popular reports of new scientific findings.

4. As citizens we need to be able to contribute to sensible policy decisions involving science. Pollution control, for example, is intermeshed with science and technology.

Such guidelines leave unanswered the big question of how much actual scientific information we need to know. Quite a lot, one would say on a common-sense basis. Yet the scholarly scientists who have worked with the schools warn that much of what we know will be wrong in a few years. Besides, they say, the amount of scientific knowledge is so great—and exploding so fast—that it is futile to try to cover it all. In every scientific discipline, they point out, there are a few fundamental concepts and generalizations that are basic to all the rest; we ought to "post-hole" deep into these and understand them thoroughly. This, along with a clear sense of the methods of inquiry and the freedom of spirit to inquire, is what really counts for the generalist. Furthermore, if basic ideas are learned, the information that they are built on will "stick" better in the mind.

The writer is neither a scientist nor a mathematician, though he has keen interests in both fields. He believes that the science/ math sector of the curriculum is in the best shape of any part of the school program. This is the result of the revolution of the late fifties and early sixties, when outstanding scholars from various fields helped schools reshape their programs. There are wonderful curricular programs available in both elementary and secondary years, programs that meet very well the guidelines suggested above if they are used properly.

There is, however, a serious problem in the upper years of high school. Up to this point there are programs that can be adapted to the needs of all students. Several programs of elementary science are genuinely dedicated to generating the spirit of inquiry and relating it to real-life problems. The new approach to geography combines real science with real humanity. At the junior high school level, the first-round treatments of both physical and biological study are keyed to what all of us need.

However, in the upper years of the senior high school, where chemistry and physics and sometimes advanced biology are the common offerings, there is little except "straight" academic programs geared to the abler students and college preparation. A minority of high school students take chemistry; only about a fifth take physics. This is simply not good enough. Not that everybody has to have traditional chemistry and physics, but all persons living in our great technology need a closer acquaintance with the physical and biological world than can be provided in the elementary and junior high school.

There is a tremendous need for simpler, less abstract offerings in the senior high—not just watered-down versions of traditional courses, but a new approach closer to the concrete realities of ordinary life and to the problems of our society. Far too many students are turning away from the natural sciences and technology. The science people need to be making the kind of effort to recapture this group with the same imagination that they used around 1960 to attract the ablest students.

In school practice there is another serious problem. A great many teachers are still teaching the new math and the new science the same way they taught the old. Science is treated as a mass of facts to be learned, rather than as an adventurous inquiry system. Math is taught as a series of computational skills rather than as a language and a way of thought. It is bad enough that this produces poorer scientists and mathematicians, but what is really tragic is that we miss the opportunity to help young learners become bold, imaginative seekers and problem solvers.

Here is one more example of the universal problem that comes from seeing a subject field as a body of information rather than as a body of purposes and goals. The details, which will mostly be forgotten anyway, get in the way of the big ideas. The potential development of the person himself is sacrificed to the acquisition of knowledge and skill he will probably never need or use. Something which could be a magnificent means to noble ends is turned into a routine end-in-itself. When we ask, "What should the schools teach?" we generally follow with the limited question, "What knowledge is of most worth?" That question has its values. But the deeper question goes un-asked, "What results, what changes—in the person, in society—are of most worth?"

DEVELOPING EFFECTIVE CITIZENSHIP

The whole business of asking inadequate questions and coming up with equally inadequate answers may be at its worst in civic education. We make a tremendous investment in the social studies; by and large, students spend more time in them than in any other field. But, in large degree, the social studies have come unhitched from anything except academic purposes, and do little to change behavior.

This is tragic, for we need effective citizens more than ever. Our American society and the whole world face a fast-climaxing series of grave problems that threaten our environment. Natural resources are being used up. In great areas explosive population growth portends disaster. There is rankling injustice to oppressed racial/ethnic minority groups and depressed social classes. Hunger, poverty, and disease strike where they are no longer unavoidable. The centers of our cities decay, while more and more people gather into huge metropolitan areas. Automobile traffic mounts to choking proportions.

Some of the problems are growing so fast and are so crucial that they must be well on the way to solution by the end of this century, or they may never be solved at all. Over everything hangs the great cloud of war and annihilation. Here in the United States, these problems rise before us at just the moment when we are less sure of ourselves and more torn by internal strife and shifting values than we have ever been before.

Clearly, the times cry out for a new level of leadership and organized action. Survival is at stake, and if the great crises can be averted at all, the job can be done only by the all-out effort of an intelligent, effective, and dedicated citizenry.

What are the great questions to ask, then, about our efforts in civic education? Don't we have to ask ourselves questions like these?

> How well have we equipped each young man or woman to help solve the problems that have to be solved? Will they be able to solve the problems we have been unable to handle? When our young people graduate, will they be devoted to the common good? How clear are their goals? How effective are they in getting things done?

But what are the questions we actually ask about the effect of our social studies? In real practice, don't we usually worry more about questions like these?

> How much do our students know about the facts of history, especially American history? How well will they do on the college entrance exams? How much do they know about the structure of our government? How good are they at geography and, possibly, economics?

The writer has been bothered for years by this substitution of informational minutiae for function. He simply refuses to excite himself very much any more about the traditional academic embellishments, not because a sound knowledge of history, government, geography, and economics is not valuable; it is. Furthermore, in each of these social disciplines—and others—the schools are obliged to start some students on the road to lofty specialized scholarship. But information in itself is only a means. The true goal is wise and ethical action in a time when there is not much margin left for error. We must have programs that will go straight to the heart of our problems.

What should the schools teach, then? Once more, the answers come hard. We have to ask ourselves first: in this great republic, with its free and democratic way of life, what really makes up the "effective citizen"? No one knows the whole answer to that, and no one should be dogmatic about it. Besides, not all citizens need to be—or should be—the same; there is an infinite variety of ways to be a good citizen, and diversity is good for our society. Still, perhaps, we can venture a few generalizations about what we need to produce if we are going to have men to match our problems.

A good citizen is sensitively aware of problems and needs. He pays attention to them. He senses them as they develop, while they are still small.

A good citizen knows how to take problems apart, analyze the contributing factors, and use data to figure out what is wrong.

A good citizen hunts for solutions, and he is both practical and idealistic about it. He studies various proposals and digs into their probable long-run effects on different groups of people and society as a whole. He weighs costs and gauges the probable cost-effectiveness of each proposition.

A good citizen is tough. He has the nerve to look serious challenges in the eye and "hang in there" for a long time, even if the situation looks almost hopeless.

A good citizen is dedicated to the good of all. He is willing to make personal sacrifices if they are necessary. He is cooperative and joins forces with others. But, at the same time, a good citizen is capable of being a rugged individualist when necessary. He can say "No" when everybody around him is saying "Yes." He is demanding of his government, seeing it as his servant who is accountable to him. In fact, he can get pretty rough at times.

A good citizen knows how to get things done. He is skillful in group action without being manipulative. He has a profound respect for every person; he can listen, and he understands group dynamics.

A good citizen is deeply ethical. He thinks through his basic values carefully. He ponders what kind of society he wants for others to live in as well as himself. And he keeps reshaping his values as he grows in wisdom.

A good citizen joins the action. He participates, doing what he can, large or small.

Quite an order! Of course, not all good citizens will be the same. We differ by temperament. Some of us enjoy the hurly-burly of direct action; others are quieter and find it hard to "mix it up." We differ in our ideas of what is desirable. We differ in all sorts of ways, so it is all right if some of us are less activist than others.

But suppose the sketch above is somewhat accurate. What kind of learning does it take to move toward development of such a citizenry. And what can the schools do?

1. Schools can change their focus. Time allotments are one key. Out of long habit, we hardly stop to think when we assign large blocks of time to topics like the Civil War. But we might be startled if we heard that some class devoted a whole semester to the problems of saving and restoring the environment or to the pressing matter of urban renewal. Maybe it ought to be the other way around; maybe we should assign time in proportion to a topic's real-life importance.

2. Schools can teach rational, systematic ways of identifying and analyzing problems, needs, and possibilities. Take, for example, the nagging problem of traffic congestion. Students today are so interested in cars that they generally sit bolt upright whenever the automobile is mentioned; they are ready to locate the roots of the traffic problem and predict the probable consequences if we continue on our present path. They can be fascinated by the technological possibilities that apparently lie just over the horizon. They can study the costs and probable effects of bigger superhighways, if we choose that route, or of various plans of rapid mass transportation. They can scrutinize what government is already doing, what proposals lie before it, how public opinion is shaping up, and what forces are at work on it.

These matters are all the real stuff of a living, pulsing society. And if the teaching is reasonably adroit, they will be learning far more than just what to do about the automobile. They will be learning to apply intelligence to social needs.

3. Schools can sensitize students to values and the value choices that lie before us. In the preceding example, the question of what will happen to people as the result of any given line of action can be kept constantly in mind. Schools and teachers should refrain absolutely from trying to dictate values, no matter how gently they do it. But they can make the questions highly visible, and they can teach reasonably objective ways of weighing the values that lie behind action choices.

4. Schools can identify and use the most powerful subject-matter media for various purposes. For instance, we have placed tremendous reliance on history to produce a wide range of ef-

fects such as "perspective;" it *is* a powerful medium, in good hands. But, for some purposes, cultural anthropology may be more effective. For example, in helping students become aware of hidden values and value conflicts in our own society, it is useful to study similar elements in other, perhaps simpler, societies. It is easier to identify these elements and become objective about them in far-away places where the emotional loading is not so high. Then the developed skills can be brought home and applied to ourselves.

Economics, sociology, political science, social psychology, and philosophy all have distinctive powers to offer. No one student can grasp them all, but key ideas and ways of thinking from each of them can be woven into the tapestry of the social studies. This is important, for we are limiting ourselves far too narrowly when we depend so heavily on history, geography, and the study of government.

5. Schools can make far greater use of the community. We have long since stopped thinking that we can teach science without laboratories, sports without playing fields, or home economics without kitchens and clothing laboratories. Now it is high time to realize we cannot teach effective citizenship without a laboratory—without getting the kids' hands dirty, so to speak.

The community is just the laboratory we need. While state and national governments are important, the individual citizen can have more influence nearer home, and students should learn to work there on small-scale, practicable projects before they move into wider circles. A community offers wide opportunities to study and work with the town board or city council, the mayor and the school board, as well as with such less official bodies as the Chamber of Commerce, the Better Business Bureau, the P.T.A., fraternal organizations, and so on. City administration includes a variety of units, such as port authorities, renewal agencies, welfare offices, courts, and various regulatory bodies; rural areas have county extension offices, soil conservation districts, water districts, and so on.

The more mature students can easily pay their way. They can make studies; communities need a lot of them. They can volunteer services in planning. Many youths would rather help build and supervise playgrounds for children than have recreation centers given to themselves. Adolescents could provide much of the labor needed in such projects as Operation Headstart, and with good adult supervision they could learn enormously from the experience. We vastly underestimate the energy and idealism of youth, and their craving to get into the act.

One part of the community that could use their help and be highly educative to them is that cluster of agencies associated with the Community Chest: the Red Cross and other health agencies, community centers, homes for the aging, settlement houses, boys' clubs, and so on. These agencies are important in the real life of a community, and youth ought to become psychologically involved in them.

6. Schools can teach directly the skills of democratic decision making and action. Students can quickly learn orderly parliamentary practice as well as the use of such facilitating devices as role playing, buzz sessions, and socio-drama. They can learn to handle disagreement and build upon it. They can be helped to listen to others and to develop sensitivity to what is going on in a group. One has only to look at the scarcity of people with such abilities in almost any adult organization to realize the need for such learning.

Furthermore, working on group problems in an open, mutually supportive setting can help each participant to understand himself better, recognize his own half-hidden motivations, and sense how his actions affect other people. Over months and years, moving gently and unobtrusively, without prying into private matters, schools could develop a wholesome and desirable self-insight and sensitivity to others.

7. Each school can use itself deliberately as a model of society and as a laboratory. Traditionally, student government, valuable as it has been, has contained a great deal of window-dressing. The students themselves have corrected this to a great extent by insisting on a real voice, and the courts have helped to define their rights.

We need not proceed so timidly in this area. To be sure, there may be some rough sessions. The course of true democracy, like that of true love, rarely runs smoothly. But children and youth have a tremendous, largely unused capacity to assume serious responsibility. A school that genuinely uses young people in all aspects of school life, including curriculum planning, would soon be a healthier, happier school, and it would teach effective citizenship in the process.

There are other possibilities, but the list is already long. In a general way, these are the kinds of things a school will need to do as it shifts purpose from merely knowing about some bodies of academic knowledge to *equipping each youngster to make a maximum contribution to solving the great problems of our society, and lifting this contribution to ever-higher levels.* Once that fundamental purpose is accepted, not only within the faculty but also throughout the community, the ways and means will be easy to find.

Nevertheless, the writer would be less than honest if he did not acknowledge a problem in all of this. While we need to go as directly as we can to the achievement of active, functioning, problem-solving citizenship, we also need to build a background of understanding in such areas as history, civics, and economics. How shall we put the two kinds of teaching together?

First, let us remind ourselves that starting with immediate, pressing problems does not shut us off from digging into the backgrounds of those problems. Thus, a class that gets into the whole complex of problems arising out of our rapidly expanding industrialization—the accelerating use of diminishing supplies of key natural resources and the dangerous climaxing of all forms of pollution—could easily go back to the roots of these problems. The students could search out the early warnings and the popular response; they could study various proposals that have come before the government and the mobilizing of influence for and against them; they could analyze the powers government now has and tentatively decide on what added powers, if any, are needed; and they could study public opinion on the subject, locally through their own efforts and nationally through the polls. In addition, a class could identify the major forces at work, move on to the costs involved and who will have to pay them, and cost out various proposed remedies. Perhaps recommendations could be developed (with, probably, minority reports).

In such a process, carried out with care in fairly generous time allotments, students would acquire more real feeling for the history of our country, for the formation of public opinion and ultimate action, and for hard, common-sense economics than they would acquire in typical courses in history, civics, and economics. One does not abandon knowledge and understanding when one focuses on today's problems. Furthermore, what is learned will be remembered because it is learned in a context that makes it mean something.

Second, it is a good idea to face up to the dawdling and waste of time in the typical program. In the usual three rounds of American history, an unconscionable amount of time is given to the Pilgrim Fathers. Hours are spent on minute details of battles and on the chronology of presidents, most of it to be forgotten after the next test. What is at all important about such chronology could be put into some form of programmed instruction, taught in less than half the time, and taught more effectively.

Still, if there must be some sacrifice of traditional information, so be it. The great goal of civic education—to develop a citizenry that will help our nation solve the enormous problems before it—is worth an even greater sacrifice. A social studies program based on solid purpose will have real life, with little resemblance to the inert fact-mongering of the present courses.

PROMOTING PERSONAL FULFILLMENT

In the final analysis, what a young person becomes is the true measure of education. Of course, schooling is only a small part of a child's real education. His family, the neighborhood he grows up in, the other young people he associates with, the church he attends: these and many other powerful influences may shape him far more than his school.

Nevertheless, the school can do a great deal. Whatever it does has to be accomplished in every nook and cranny of the school's program. This includes the whole climate of the school—on the playground, in athletics, and hobby clubs, as well as in every subject matter field, in home economics and shop, in the math and sciences and the social studies, and in basic areas of the language arts.

Still, especially if we think of "becoming" in terms of the growth of inner qualities, there is one part of the curriculum that has special opportunities. This is the humanities. The humanities, sometimes spoken of as humanistic studies, are hard to define, partly because any worthwhile field can be taught to contribute to humanness. Certainly the sciences—and surely history—can be a powerful study of humanity. But a few fields have special resources.

In recent years many secondary schools have begun developing unified humanities programs to pull together the resources of several media into a single powerful "study of man." They take their content from a variety of fields, but three bases are almost universal:

Art—Including architecture, photography, and the motion picture as well as the usual drawing and painting

Music—Including work from all times and places

Literature—Including poetry, drama, the novel, biography, and many varieties of nonfiction.

(This writer feels that for a genuine study of man students need psychology and cultural anthropology, because these represent a great new means of studying humanity. So far, however, use of these aids is rare.) Altogether, this movement toward the humanities may be the most important curriculum development of our times.

But this is getting ahead of our story. A good curriculum worker should not start with subject matter, but with purpose. After all, the purpose here is not just to teach more about art, music, and literature; the purpose is to *help each young person as much as we can in his own personal becoming.*

To do that we first have to ask, what do we want young people to become? That is, once more, what are our purposes? Of course, we do not want all students to be the same; in fact, we want the highest measure we can get of true individuality. Still, we can identify a few great universals to which most people would agree. One way to do this is to look at the young person from several different angles. For example, most of us, just on a common-sense basis, would probably like him to have simple goodness of character. If asked to spell that out, we might use words like honor, integrity, honesty, decency, and generosity.

A religious leader surely would want those qualities. But, from his special view of life, he might wish to emphasize reverence, compassion, a clear sense of ethical values, and commitment to something greater than self.

A prospective employer might stress still different words, even though he would agree with those above. He might add reliability, willingness to take responsibility, cooperativeness, and loyalty.

Teachers from various fields might add special qualities. A coach might stress fair play. A social studies teacher might add a clear sense of social values and commitments. An artist or musician might stress a love of beauty, sensitivity, and creativity. A scientist would almost surely add commitment to truth. Regardless of field, graduate school professors ·would probably value qualities like a free spirit of inquiry, independence, and persistence in working on a tough problem.

Psychologists have special ways of looking at the structure of a personality. They may think in terms of a healthy personality or a fully functioning person. When they analyze that, they use terms like openness and warmth, life-seekingness, autonomy (to be one's own person), the urge to communicate, the ability to love and be loved, self-insight and self-acceptance, understanding and acceptance of others, and the ability to stand stress and uncertainty.

The list is not complete, but it need not be. We all have some image of the kind of person we would like to become and to help other people become. We all know that we are in the area of the most important thing in life. Then the question is, what can we do about it, in school? More specifically, what can the humanities do?

To begin to answer that, we should look first at the resources we have; they are tremendous. On the one hand, we have literature and all the arts. This great treasure house is the record of all mankind's aspirations and yearnings, troubles and frustrations, and doubts and beliefs. The great intuitive geniuses of all times and places have given voice to their deepest insights. They have seldom been far from the problems of the lonely human soul and the always unsatisfying social order.

It is true that we often read books, listen to music, or look at paintings simply to pass the time pleasantly. It is also true, unfortunately, that schools have used such works—often spoken of as classics—with major attention to form and technique, and little ear for what they have to say. And yet we have all been formed far more than we know by the occasional poem, play, or motion picture that spoke to the center of our being. This is an intimately personal thing; the song which moves you deeply may be only a casual tune to your neighbor. The movie that shakes up your neighbor may have been only two hours of entertainment to you.

Yet, underneath this, we are all alike. Our sense of beauty stems largely from the words and works of those who see what we would never see without them. Our ideals have been shaped not only by the great literature of religion, but also by the drama and the novel. We understand ourselves and others and identify with the universal human condition because we have shared the insights of sculptors, playwrights, and poets.

If this seems overdrawn, one has only to consider how greatly the mind, not only of black America but of all America, has been changed by a handful of black writers in a couple of decades. One has only to look at how greatly the value patterns of young America are shaped by the writers of popular songs. The powers are there; we have only to learn to use them creatively with young people.

Another body of resources lies in what are commonly called the behavioral sciences. These—psychology and cultural anthropology, especially—are almost peculiarly a landmark of the twentieth century. They have opened up a direct, scientific search into the nature of man, his motivations, and his potentials. They add enormously to our ability to understand and live with ourselves and others. And they, too, in their way, have enriched our vision of what human beings can be and do. Such writers as the famous psychologist, Carl Rogers, have held before our eyes the realistic possibility that men and women will function at a level rarely achieved. The potentials they reveal are so powerful we hardly dare to believe that our children have them. The schools have, thus far, virtually ignored this second set of resources, largely because so few teachers are prepared to handle them.

Of course, bookish resources are not all we have. For some children—perhaps for all—real experience has unique power. If we wish our young people to develop a sense of compassion, perhaps the best thing is to get them opportunities to help little children, the poor, and the aging.

Now, how can we mobilize these powerful forces and let them do their great work inside each youngster? First, we must remind ourselves that this is an intensely personal area. Not all boys or girls will necessarily resonate to the same pieces of art or literature. There is no reason why they should have to. Second, we must remind ourselves—again and again—that it is not our basic purpose to have all students learn some preselected body of classics. Our job is to help each child or youth find those things that speak to his heart, and then help him listen.

This will call for extremely artistic teaching. It will demand a team of teachers with varied traits and talents, operating in a highly open and flexible situation. Suppose we try to visualize a humanities laboratory, with such a team of teachers in an open-space arrangement. The furnishings are homelike and comfortable, with little resemblance to a traditional classroom. The furniture is grouped into conversational interest centers, changeable at will. Books and magazines lie about, and works of art are displayed. High fidelity recordings of fine music—including present-day music—are there in large collections, to be listened to sometimes by large groups but more often through private headphones.

The great motion pictures are available, again to be viewed sometimes by all, but more often self-selected by two or three students to be viewed in desk-size projection with earphones. Prints and transparencies of great art will be abundant. In alcoves there will be facilities for students who want to "mess around," trying their hand at composing a song, perhaps, or making a poster.

It will be a tranquil, rather leisurely place, very different from the crisp intellectual organization of a science class. It will be characterized, more than anything else, by arrangements for good conversation. Sometimes the groupings will be large, even, on request, large enough for a lecture. But more often threes and fours and half-dozens will get together to discuss themes of common interest, perhaps developing out of their readings or other studies. The subject will be life itself.

Why this rather fanciful description of a laboratory that probably exists nowhere on earth, though it easily could exist? The writer is stretching his imagination in order to make a point. If we wish to achieve certain results, the means we use must fit the expectation. We do not try to teach football by asking questions about a textbook chapter. Why do we think we can help youngsters clear up their values by examining the details of *Silas Marner*?

Young people today need a chance to get acquainted with themselves, deep down inside. They need to try on for size many different kinds of ideas. They need perspective to see that the human problems they are wrestling with are old in time, though perhaps different in form. They need to become aware of the shining visions of the best of the world's thinkers, dreamers, and moral leaders. They need time to test these ideas, largely by talking about them with their peers. But it is not good enough that these talks be empty bull-sessions, the sharing of ignorance. Students need the help of teachers to find what is of value to them, teachers to sharpen the questions and the focus and help them dig far beneath the surface. They need counselors who know more about this world than they do.

For all this, there is no other medium which is even in the same class with the arts and literature and the behavioral sciences. Here it is that the great questions of values—of life itself and its significance—are raised. Here it is that the great heroes of mankind stand before our eyes. Here it is that the finest in man is set alongside everything that is tawdry and sleazy. There are "answers," too, the solutions as they have been seen by this man or that woman. Perhaps these answers are, in a way, less important than the clear portrayal of the questions. It is a great service simply to get the great problems and choices out into the open where they can be thought about and talked about.

The typical teaching of literature and art and music misses the point. It is too technical, not human enough. We need not so much to teach a few great works as to use what speaks to us in our day. Abraham Lincoln said a man could worry himself into obscurity, protecting his own interests, or forget himself into immortality. Jesus said the Sabbath was made for man, and not man for the Sabbath. Schools, likewise, can worry themselves into futility in an endless concern for putting across bits and pieces of information; they can act as if the relative greatness and the technique of a literary work are more important than the response of the reader—as if man was made for Shakespeare, not Shakespeare for man. Schools can fritter away their power on academic fanciness. But the great human problems go on, to be solved—where? on the street corner? at a Friday night party?

This is not an easy time for a boy or a girl to be growing

up—as parents know. Our young people enjoy few of the old certainties. They have little chance to grow up "naturally" in a stable order of things. Everything is changing around them. Everything is under new scrutiny, new questioning. For many of them—rightly or wrongly—the old religion, the old social ideals, the old matter-of-fact assumptions about how to live are not enough.

They face questions, far more questions than any youngster should have to answer on his own. They face threats, ominous signs that the physical world and society are headed for disaster in their lifetime. But also, in vague, intuitive ways, they catch fleeting visions of a better world. They follow the gleams eagerly, anxiously, often restlessly. They move faddishly from one "solution" to another, and too many of them "burn out" in a few feverish years.

They need our help, not to give them the answers for we do not have those answers ourselves. But we do have the great resources of all men's insight; we do have systematic ways of posing the great questions of life and working at them. The opportunity to work humbly, shoulder-to-shoulder with our young people, groping our way toward new understanding, faith, and commitment is what the unified humanities program has to offer.

A REFLECTION

As I look back over these pages, I know that I will have disturbed many by my relative lack of emphasis on traditional knowledge and skills. I do believe most deeply that young men and women must come out from our schools competently equipped with ample resources of useful, organized information and know-how. What I have not had space—or the ability—to show is how much knowledge and skill will be encountered —and used—in the course of such a program as I have advocated. My own estimate is that knowledge and skill will prosper in such a curriculum.

But, be that as it may, I cannot back down from my insistence that much of the knowledge we now labor so hard to put across is not worth the candle. It is inert, deadwood; it only lies there and looks pretty. Compared to the great purposes that could inform every day's efforts, it is, to be blunt about it, simply trivial.

What we need is a return to the old ideal of a liberal education—the most magnificent conception of education ever to spring from the mind of man. I define it simply as education which uses organized content, drawn from high in the culture, but uses it always in the making of a human being. Toward that fulfillment the great essentials are readiness for a fine lifetime career, effectiveness as a citizen, and, above all, enrichment of the inner self to its full potential.